Poppy Tears

Manal Hamed

authorHOUSE®

AuthorHouse™ UK
1663 Liberty Drive
Bloomington, IN 47403 USA
www.authorhouse.co.uk
Phone: 0800.197.4150

Published by AuthorHouse 01/09/2016

ISBN: 978-1-5049-9758-4 (sc)
ISBN: 978-1-5049-9757-7 (hc)
ISBN: 978-1-5049-9759-1 (e)

Contents

Fleeting serendipity

Humming bird In a book About to escape
The wings flutter, The eyes
Delate..Being So small
Made it easier. Buzzing as it Freed itself
From the old crumbling pages
Humming bird Near a flower
Sipping nectar. Happily; I wonder How it hovers
And will hover still.
Freedom suits it well. Iridescent colors..
Indigo. Green Patches of red,
Some white too. Making its way to another flower..

Humming bird pin; To adorn A cotton
T- Shirt Yet...still as it Is,. Beauty is in every corner
In Frida's* paintings as well
Fleeting serendipity Fearless, Fragile; delicate. Bee-size bird
Humming bird in a book
Beside it Scrippled:'The joy of the heart"
Coming from no-where!

*Frida Kahlo

Poppy tears.

Tears of a poppy'
dripping; so.
They say..
They contain opium
Those fragile red.
Fluttering petals..
A dark stem
Bearing a red cup..
Sylvia Plathe liked
Them.
I looked at the poppies
Not in a field
Of some French impressionist painter
In my face-book
Page..
You sent me some..
Do I like you?
Do you like me..?
The eternal question
Posed..
In the wrong moment.
I looked at the dancing
Poppy..
Dews collect
Slip
And recollect
As my memories
Of you..
"Stupid"
You called me once..
Why send a stupid
Girl
Poppies..?

Chrysalis..

Few droplets..
Dancing
In the sun
Flickering..
Shimmering.
Shining like smooth pearls.

Wings of a butterfly
About
To stretch.

Extend your wings"
My blue butterfly..
Shine
As you kiss the
Flowers of spring..
Chrysalis..
You appealed
Before
To the man of my dreams..
Chrysalis.
I remained too
Fossilized for years..
Waiting
Your dewy male touch..//
I dreamt of you..
Will you flutter..?
And collect the nectar
Of my blossoming
Jasmines?
Or is it the illusion of a poetic
Fantasy?

Why did the bird flew

To Egypt crumbling..

Things around me
Fall apart..
Bullets shot at night
Explosives defused..
This is not the place
I was born
In..
Wishing for souvenirs
To come back
My college years..
The innocence of
being a dreamy
Poet..
The smile at reciting a
Poem..
A trembling flower in-between
My forgotten book
Half read.
The phobia before an exam..
Who would have thought..
That I may long for
all this things..
Amidst a country
That has lost its soul..
The torment..
Of not knowing what to come..
The shedding of tears..
The fuming skies..
The death
Of young hopes. young girls.
For merely daring to
critise an older
Generation..
Fossiled.as they are..

With their wrinkled eyes..
Their rigid..
Unpromising steps..
The birds that chant heedless
Of the bullets to come..
I envy the birds
Their calmness..
Their freedom and
Their childhood ecstasy
At the sight of water..
Their dance among
The flowers of spring..
I envy you your courage
My friend..
The honest..
Summation of our past..
The insight..
The revelations..
Of a..a leftist journalist..
I pine in my hesitation..
The torment..
Of a hidden female..
I regret..
My years..
My tears spilt.
Over disputes of work
Today the sun will shine..
And we never knew who killed
Who..
And why the land crumbled.
Why the rain dropped..
Why the swallow flew?

The Spiral

With every word
    That you say
    You steal
    My heart away
…
My soul
    More and more
    Without any blame
  Or
Critical remarks..
You steal

My thoughts
And more
    The poems
Are no longer sufficient

To forget you
    Because
It is around them
That I dance..!

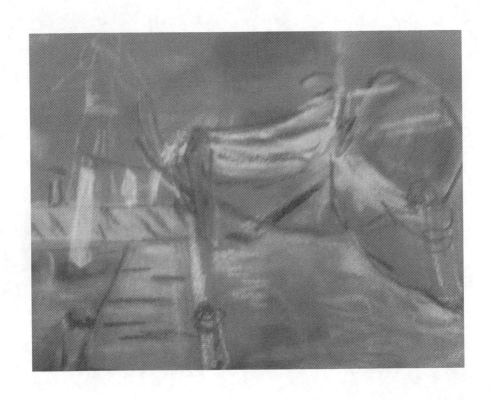

Curfew!

Forgive me
There are no ink
Not any more..
Because
I have thrown the ink pot
To the sea
And the feather
In the air
The feathers fly
Wither
My soul with them too
The photographs
Are in the papers
No justice still
Nothing
To color the life
With the green color..
I am no longer that blind lover
The imaginative poet
With twinkling eyes
I am no poetess
I confess
No poems can
Express
The emptiness
Of withering flowers..
I cannot even buy the
Papers of tomorrow
Because of the curfew..

Your moon

The rays of the moon..
Your inspirative shots..
Soon..
The flickering sadness..
The grey zone..
Of..your ideologies..
I knew such a moon.
I knew the color of madness.
The apples thrown to the sea..
The bottles with
Love notes
Hid amidst the waves..
The flowers dried
Awaiting
The frame..
Of your hands
To adorn them..
I knew of such hopes too..
Only..
I was never that brave..
The moon..
In your eyes ..
Is lovelier than the moon in the
Sky!

Nothing to do

Idleness; nothing to do
except perhaps
pretending to watch the news
nothing much

people tormenting others

People

pretending they know it all

having a name for all

categorizes

"Immigrants"
"Civil war"
"Curfew""

"loans"
"peace"

                        nothing but
a destructive force at work

Why we hide our inhumanity
When it slaps us in our face?

wrens singing

Wrens do sing
just like any other bird
    they may be fat and brown
not seen amongst the brown leaves

yet they do have sweet voices
just like fat girls

    only we see the brownness in hem
and overlook the songs!

smuggled sadness

You are lurking in the shadows
Of my screen; with hairs so clear
And eyes that glean with desire
A man? a small nightmarish dream
both;? may be -I stare; and The glare
    from the screen; Prevents me from seeing clearly
I cannot really know
Why you added that photo of
A girl missing ; disappearing On 25th of October
That is my birthday ; I sign out
I close the laptop and the ink spilt
Spilling still from my buttons
Dripping...Drip —drip drip- drop
No; this is not another
Steven King's novel; Or Pram Stoker's Dracula
In the phantasmagoria; Of the swiping browsers
I am lost' reading all about your
Ex-lovers; The girls you left behind
Cities you visited... the Monalisa smile
On your face; what a face!

That care- free dubious smile; Don Juan ' I told you once
And your victims crying
In silence; Or pretending to go on
With their lives and here I am
On the other shore of the Mediterranean
That is exploding; Of war-Torn apart
Evacuated as it were; The aftermath of another failing
Affair... You see I once
Foolishly wrote a poem
About you ; even a whole anthology; Entitled " poppy tears"
With black seeds; Hiding yellow specks
Of colour; waving in the breeze
Awaiting your touch
Dripping sadness
From their opiate capsules

I felt so poetic; Still in that haze of fantasy
Only to wake up to reality; Your monstrosity
With her wearing same
Identitical T.shirt- I had no right to stealthy look..
"tick- tock"..Tick tick...yes I happened to notice
The grey hair creeping
In my otherwise brown tresses
Hers was done a la mode; Like you liked it perhaps..
Free-, modern ...she even celebrated your
Birthday with you while
Greece was being sliced by
Germany..
The feast for the macabre: In some ...Europe modern..
I kept reading for two days about Greek mythology
"monster ! monster!" as you really were
Gallic charm bewitches us all
I felt like a refugee that day
Only I Had no smuggler to smuggle my sadness!

Poppy seeds

Done with the tears..
Will the seeds grow?
I have to be
Patient..
They keep
Telling me..
Mushrooming
Poppies inn
My paintings
You see
How i miss thee?

three roses
on canvass
still

well

I repainted the

painting

like
the way Matisse
did
    when he
had
not much money

to buy
a new white canvass
on the window
sill
there was a sparrow

chirping
as it built its nest

you too
were

  putting tables

one by one

  I admired it

via facebook
telling you
I loved wood
so

fooling myself
you are still alone

only to discover after
I narrow-escaped a bomb

that she was the reason of
that beaming smile of yours..
alas...birds were

  only
making me more patient
and accompanying me in my loneliness..!

To humming birds again

at last
I saw you
in my dream
you crossed the oceans
the poem
that hear your name
at last once more they
nominate me a poet-ess.

and all the difference it makes
for me
poetry
is a bless
Yes
A curse too
they always liked the poetess
never the woman...
at last
my hovering humming bird has found its
favourite flower
however
you said nothing
a Pygmalion story unfolds
I revolt
you recoil not believing
your statuette
have an opinion too!

Dew

Eye
tears

like dew

falling

Where are you?

Will l spend my lifetime
searching for
you still?

too weak to resist

you like strong women...

you do..

Dew

attracts only the wind!

Orchids

I told you before
you look like an iris
smiling
in the same way
those rainbows-like petals do
I am
someone
who happens to like flowers
I guess
most poets and painters
do..
you see we cannot helps
it fragile
and liable to break we seem

I think
you may one day read this
if you do
remember me
and think how many
dews were shed
because of you!

Uncanny

Well
I cannot tell another boring story of
a poetic girl
who believed too much in love

it is just that
I used to chase butterflies
thinking one day
I may trap them
in my lap
then let
them
free
once more
it is so eerie..

that
expression on your face
as if you are discovering me for the first time

see
I am not
that dreamy girl any more
I pretend to be
just to hang on my former self
you smiled
at me
but that lovely sweet beseeching smile of before
well
I know
times are difficult
tell me again; once more
are those poppies for real?
Or are you only enjoying
yourself
at my expenses?!

Cobalt blue

They categorize
Colors
According to mood.
I told you
Orange
Can mix
With lavender
In a parrot
I saw
You told me
So unreal
You said so,
While
You go on
Singing with
Every
Female parrot
You see,
Why
Reserve
The bitterness for me?

Anemone

Under two white
Flowers..
O'Keefe
Was
Sad
Tormented
By jea
Ousy...
The entire search
For new
Flowers
Was invoked
By her
Love
For a poppy..
All the isolation
A question
To God
Why
Give
Me love
And
Pain at the same
Time..
Deserted
Heart
Is
Weary..
Eyes
Withered
From tears
Unseen..
Being
A strong
Women
Made he travel

To the uncharted
Courses...
Counting the stars..
Arranging the petals..
One after the other
Chronicling
Het life
in the language
Of flowers
only the stupid
See
It as art..
Never second guessing
what lies
in a woman's
Heart..
Anemone
The new love
that lured
Her husband
Away
From her..
Separating the two
White
Flowers...
Still
they see the artist
And never the woman...

No Hammurabi's Bagdad

Hammurabi

need not
make all this fuss
to unite
the shards of Iraq
nor did he
resort to the un.
To undo
the errors

he simply acted..
Collapsing after him
as it did now..
what a fake illusion is that American..

Aid!

Troubled Nile wiping Euphrates

They
mapped you

calling you names
while you pierced the same

continent
river Nile..

Competing the Amazon..
..
They just couldn't
be content
to let you flow

then

also
too
caused Euphrates
to bear the wiping
of another

civilized nation

why so?

Tender iris

Your eyes will
gape
like iris petals
bees won't know if you invite
them
or
just
wait for dew..
You
as tender as
an orange iris!

The color of sadness

They
sell you
tubes
of every shape
no one yet has know the best shade
for tears
some will add
a dab of greys
others
black
some tinted
red
rose
petal
where dews
has falling
dripping
silently
like some girl's silent
grief

at a friend's betrothal
at a n interview
in a bureau
where some assole harresses
here and she tried

to hold herself

some will describe

some new

medication

To lessen anxiety
without
blaming men

some will hang
lovely
certificate
in some pedantic psychiatrist's
room
some
will tell her
it is your fault

no one
will tell her how to paint
sadness
yet when they see her painting
they have felt
it..
without
knowing the reason!

Blue butterfly

Spot
   it

   on a
yellow
   primrose

My first

   muse

if you well

   I am no bookworm

Still

poetry

floods
whenever

   I see

A butterfly

    Basking in the sun and
a finch
about
    to play with haystacks

gone

are the days
 when books fascinated me...

yet

    all

the twigs
tress
branches
know me!

I am the poetess
in disguise

mimicking
a sparrows
song

I am
the frog near
the brook

the ant crawling
to catch its food

I am
the silent dew
about to fall

I am the melodious

hiss
of autumnal
leaves..
The bluebells
scattering
all along
and the
jasmine scent
after

it has withered..

I am..
The distilled honey

of million roses!
Just
you don't see
nor figure it out!

Marigold

I wish..
I could..
Do
    As the Mexicans do
Spreading
    Marigolds
Orange
Yellow..
Lovely
    To

Celebrate
An event
    No one normally celebrates..
Marigolds..
    What a flower..
      You..
    My lovely rebel

Loved kalo...
      Gave me poppies..
Yet

How can we be lovers?

It is not meant
To be
That is why I cry in silence..
Tell me..
    How many poem
    I may write..
How many tear..
To shed
Anew..
?.
Marigolds..
    For people who leave
The agonies
Of the world..
    Hanging poppies..
    For love
    Between sky
And earth..
    Tell me...
Do you love me still
with my melancholic temper?

Figuring me out

Just a

lazy

girl

who opted for fiction
instead of being real...

just another dreamy spirit
who lit a small
candle
amidst
neon lights

time has changed
me recoiling in a grey
off-white cocoon..
you had no time to see
the butterfly that is
to grow..
Just another

girl

whose life
is so mundane
she make-up things to let days pass- by!

Intermittent clouds

Dispersing

    to collect

collecting
to disperse
white wavy
clouds...
autumn at last..!

Birds

Wings spreading
me
writing
reading may be
feeling
scattered..
Listening to birds
how could they find love so easily
how I never found it..?
looking at you

different
care free..
Spontaneous too..

Heedless of others
opinion..

Confident..

me languishing
always in
..

Self blame...
me..Wanting thousand times
to see you
your eyes
again hear your laughter
that pains me soul..
You can never
really know what is in the heart of
someone like me...
may be..?
,may be not..
tell me..
..
You see it in my eyes..
No more...?
I knew you loved manga

Me
only writing as you told me
working
lonely
lonelier still..
why i entertain a vague hope?
Why...the torment?

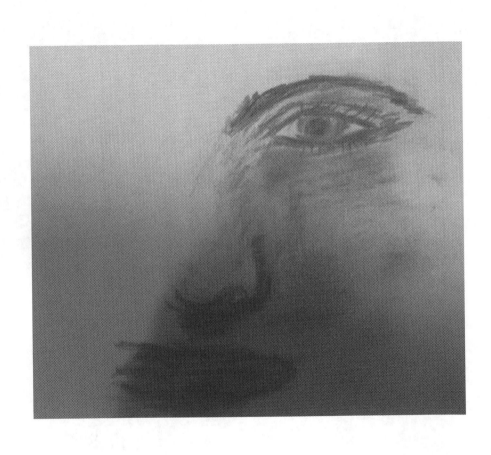

Tinted smell

Purple
 will remind
me of violets..

Red

of roses

Pink of peonies..
brown

of your eyes!

Obsessed

By
you

   an idea.

Of you

that turned out

too good to be true..

Obsessed by a tickling voice..

A faraway glance..

A word you said and hid..

A reality that

was so shocking to bear..
Obsessed by my obstinacy

female curiosity

folly..

Spontaneity...

obsessed by a dream

that is disturbing and.. Enjoyable..

The idea of love ..Always haunted me..
Like a gothic mantra..
Yet

you make it fade..
And recess
in the background of my

pathetic life

May be

One day

things will
be different

sun

will be blue..
Your eyes

will
be green

mine

with a different hew..

I will be stronger.

You will grow

fonder..!
May be!

Bookshelf in a city where electricity is cut off

Why we love?
A title..
painting
another title
doodling
third title
cashier to pay
money to squander
on books
to say
we Egypt
are civilest still..
Yes "are"
with a big a
in it
coming home
power- shut
people gunning one another
near zeitoun station
Yes
books
on my shelf
I smile
to my self
what is the use
of books now
of civilsation?
Borges was right!

sketching

Birds
　　so

May be
I' ll
learn
from
　　them

　　　how
to
fly
　　in
the

　skies
of poetry..

A wing
fluttering
A cooing of a dove
A finch
searching
for a small
grain
not a move
　　from my part
Lest the
bird
will fly
in their
　　little hearts
they

do know how
　　man is cruel!

Wagtail

Near
The metro..
Not afraid..
The tail
Goes
Up
And down
My frown
Eases
Into
A smile..
Like
You..
Your tail
Too..
Lovely
Bird
Sensing
My loneliness.
Wagging
Away
My sadness..

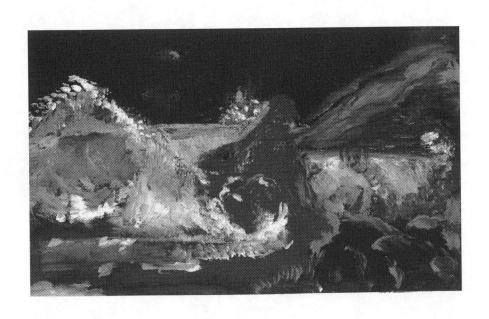

War Zone

middle east

a crime
scene
for
news.
an abode
for us..
torment
cannot be screened
you know
they hide
corpses
with a white sheet
only..
channels
wish to
uncover
the hideous
sights..
middle-est
to her is nothing
middle in it!

Meandering

In
    the maze
    of poetry
trying
to trace
the map of
love..
I need not
any gaps
It is all written
In here
    in my heart..
that is
why it do hurt..
meandering..
as I listen to your words
texted..
retraced
in my mind..
write..
instead

of self destruction..
absorbing the
wisdom
only too late..
wish I met you sooner
wish I was younger
happier
little bitter..
wish I was
in another
time all together,
darer
wish I told you then
how I loved you
instead of dabbling
in a vain
talk
about cinema!

Dying

You stood near her..
Like a bird..
Who found finally
Its suitable bird..
Me dying of grief.
I remained
Unseen..
Withering
Like an ancient
Jasmine..
Weeping as a willow.
Walking in the streets..
In Ramadan
Tired with heavy head..
Soup of lentils restored
Me a little..
Is it because she is thinner?
Blonde..with red man7cured
Awful hands she laid on you
As if claiming her territory..
You were hers then..
Me..
Sipping the remaining tears..
Smiling in self mockery..
Me..
Envying het freedom
Her blue tight dress
That made you desire her..
All my poems never
Made that effect on you..
Me..
Hating me..
And
D the worst think..
It was because
Of you...!!!

Why Liking You...

Frenchman..
You..
Were
Learning
Arabic..
And you
Approached
Me
The way birds
Do..
I felt
Certain
Liking
To you.
Historian
Then say..
You..
Told them
You are a writer..
A journalist and may be entrepreneur

All wrapped in none

You made me
A poet..
A
N
Essayist..
A translator.
Yet..
You said
Later..
You don't
Know me..
Why..
Banishing
Me from the frame...?
You
Saw
Nothing
But the beginnings
Of a bud..
The flower in full
Bloom
Startled you..
And like
All men
You refused..
To
Acknowledge
Its coming
Of age...

Purple Moon..

I liked the moon..
You shot..
Not knowing
Where
You will
Land next..
Too swift
You are for me..
Idiotic
I am..
You.
Seem
To read history..
And me..
Caged..
In my..
Obstinacy
Your moon

Hypnotized me..
Mauve.
Blurring..
Up there..
In poetic
Simplicity..
I told you
Money counts more now.
You became angry..
In due time..
You will learn..
How true..
I am..
Only..
You are young
Still
Dreamy..
I was once there too
Searching..
For a muse..
Do forget my
Cynicism,

Painted Poppies..in a clinic

I thought him
A different man..
The psychiatrist..
Who prescribed
Tegretol..
To combat my
Swinging mood..
Or whatever..
They do..
To.
Hush
Down
Creativity..
He too
Had painted
White poppies.
Hung on his wall
I wanted to ask
Him
Was his heart
Once
Broken too?

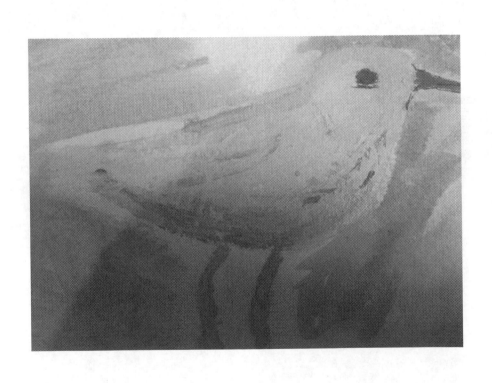

Merry- go -round

Life
is but
a circle
up
and down
to and fro
smile here
smile there
lovely wind
you go
I saw
you
for a while
merry-go -round
you like toys too
I like the same things you admire
pigeons too
i told you
we look alike
then
at the first
chance you chose someone else
merry go round
dreams are blown
the music
in my heart
is no more

Manga girl

little strands of hair
moving
tresses..
flying..
tears
on her face
she dares
say what
I cannot say
losing
the shyness
in me.
I drew her..
just as I
tried to learn
forgetting you

In spite of refusal slips

Sylvia persisted..
Yes..
Dying in poetry..
Breathing poetry..
Following the horizon..
Alienated..
Exiled..
Following the untrodden path..
Only she
Believed too
Much
In fairytales
Ad prince charming..
A love that will
Last..
She wrote..
Feminizing Lazarus..
Are all women..
Thus..
Marginalized.?
I will write..
Even if..
Poems like poppies..
Dry..
Their dewy words
Betray.
The rhythmic sobs..
Of my heart..
Even if..

You won't read me..

The rainbow in my skies.
May not last..
Yet..
Petals keep..
Whispering their scent..
Even after withering..

Blue Bells

As young..
Tried to memorize roses names..
One rose meant
To me a lot..
A poppy hung
Between the sky
And the earth..
You loved blue
Flowers so..
Why had it ended before
It even
Begun?
Me musing about you..
Me publishing
For you
To read..
You promised me promises unkempt..
Like bluebells scattered
In my soul..
Hole in my heart
That grew..
You no longer see
Dews..
On the petals
I drew..
I thought you were
Different..
I screw..

Poppies are red...

As it is well-known
    Their petals swirling in the wind
The promise of beauty
Reborn
When offered in affection
A bee will come to search
For nectar
Buzzing ; a painter
For inspiration; a poet
For a line of verse..
You for an excuse to initiate a conversation
They said I wined
Pined while shedding my verses
As a poppy that shed its tears
Ridding itself of its seeds
Yet aren't seeds the promise of a new rose
To be?
Poppies are blue too..
I am no longer sad; *for* poppies are white and yellow too.
Beckoning and smiling

Printed in the United States
By Bookmasters